Bridges

Written by
Jill Atkins

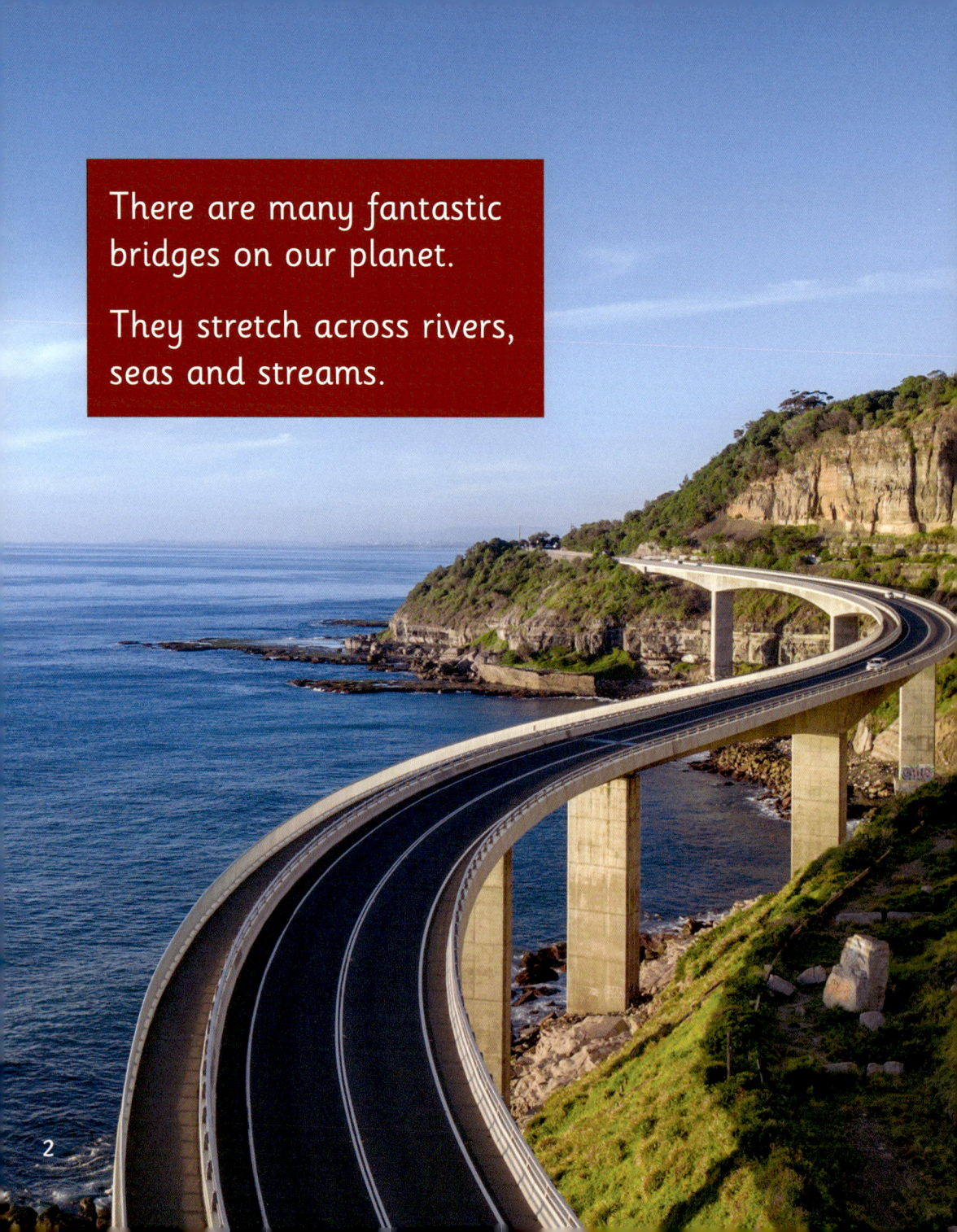

There are many fantastic bridges on our planet.

They stretch across rivers, seas and streams.

Bridges come in all shapes and sizes. They can be made of wood, stone, metal, rope or even glass.

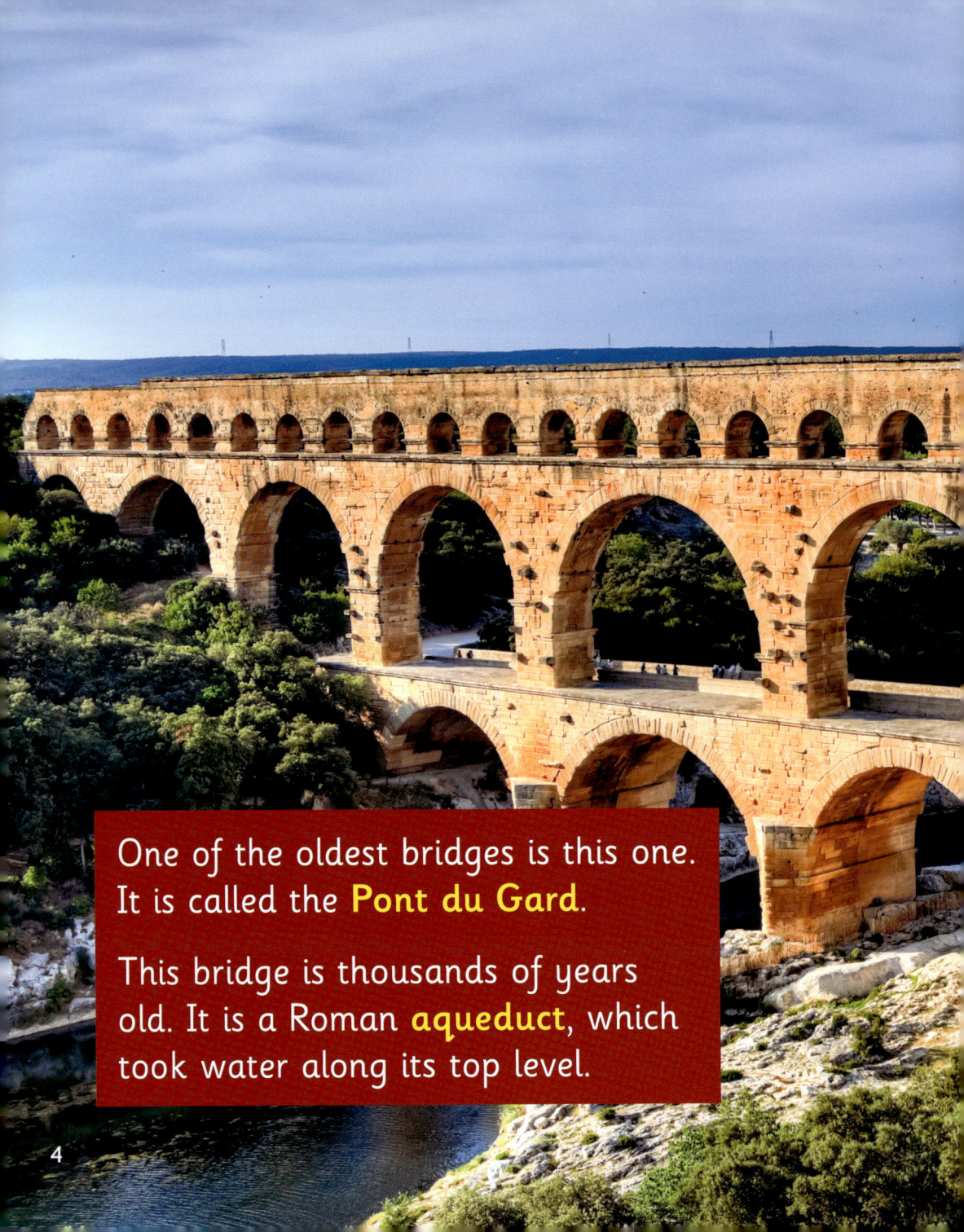

One of the oldest bridges is this one. It is called the **Pont du Gard**.

This bridge is thousands of years old. It is a Roman **aqueduct**, which took water along its top level.

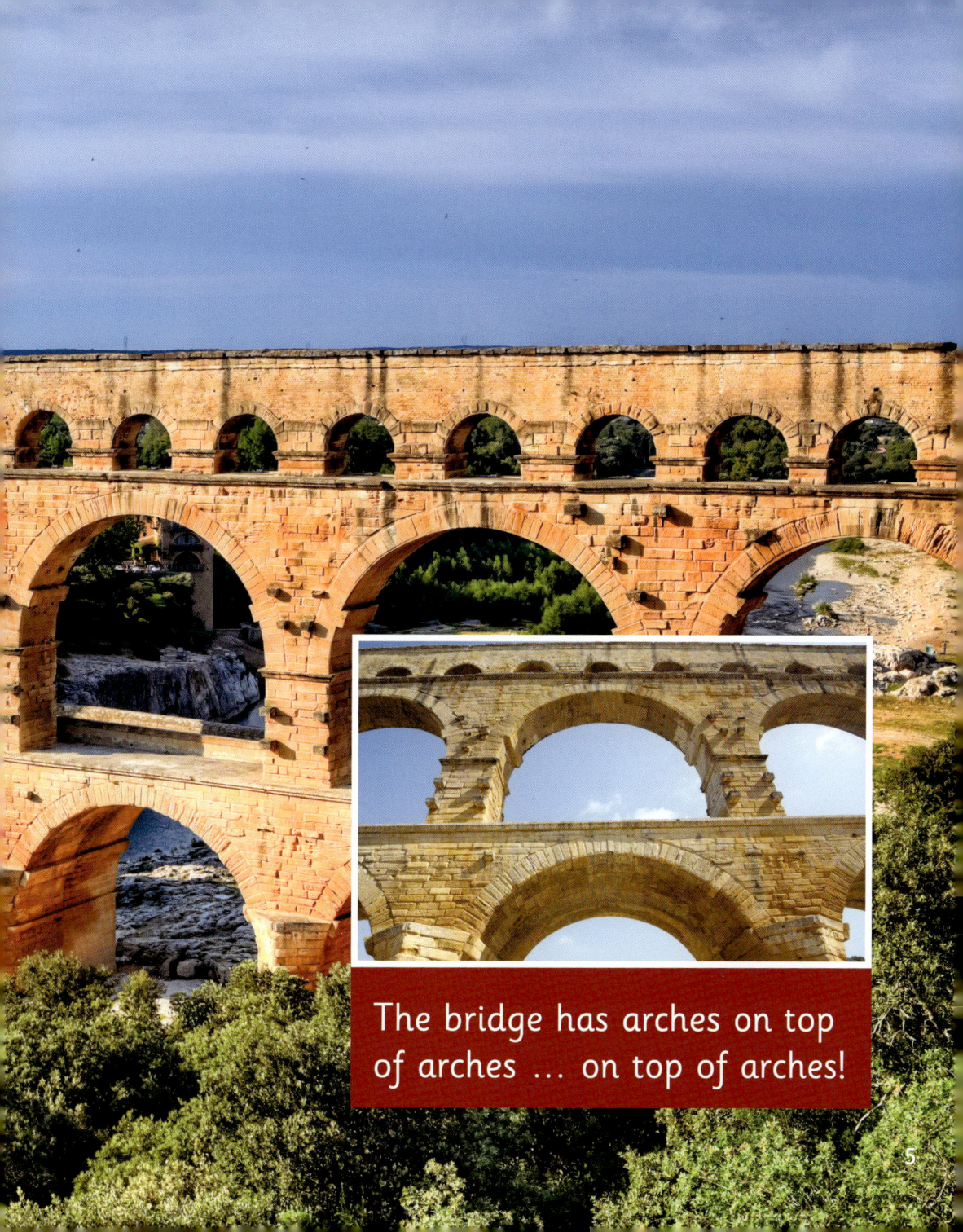

The bridge has arches on top of arches ... on top of arches!

This bridge is in Italy. It is old too.

There's a row of shops on the bridge. Many people go there to get jewels, pottery, fudge, ice cream and leather gifts.

This city in Italy has many canals instead of roads, so it is full of bridges.

This is **Tower Bridge**. It was completed over one hundred years ago.

It has a tower at each end. Can you see the high gangways along the top? You can climb up inside the towers and go along these.

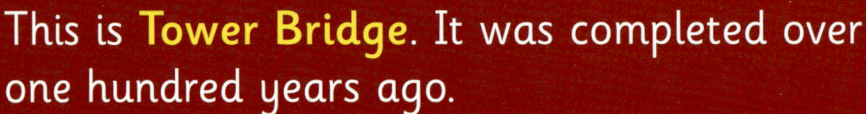

The lower part is a road, but it can be raised if a tall ship needs to pass underneath.

Can you see how this picture is different?

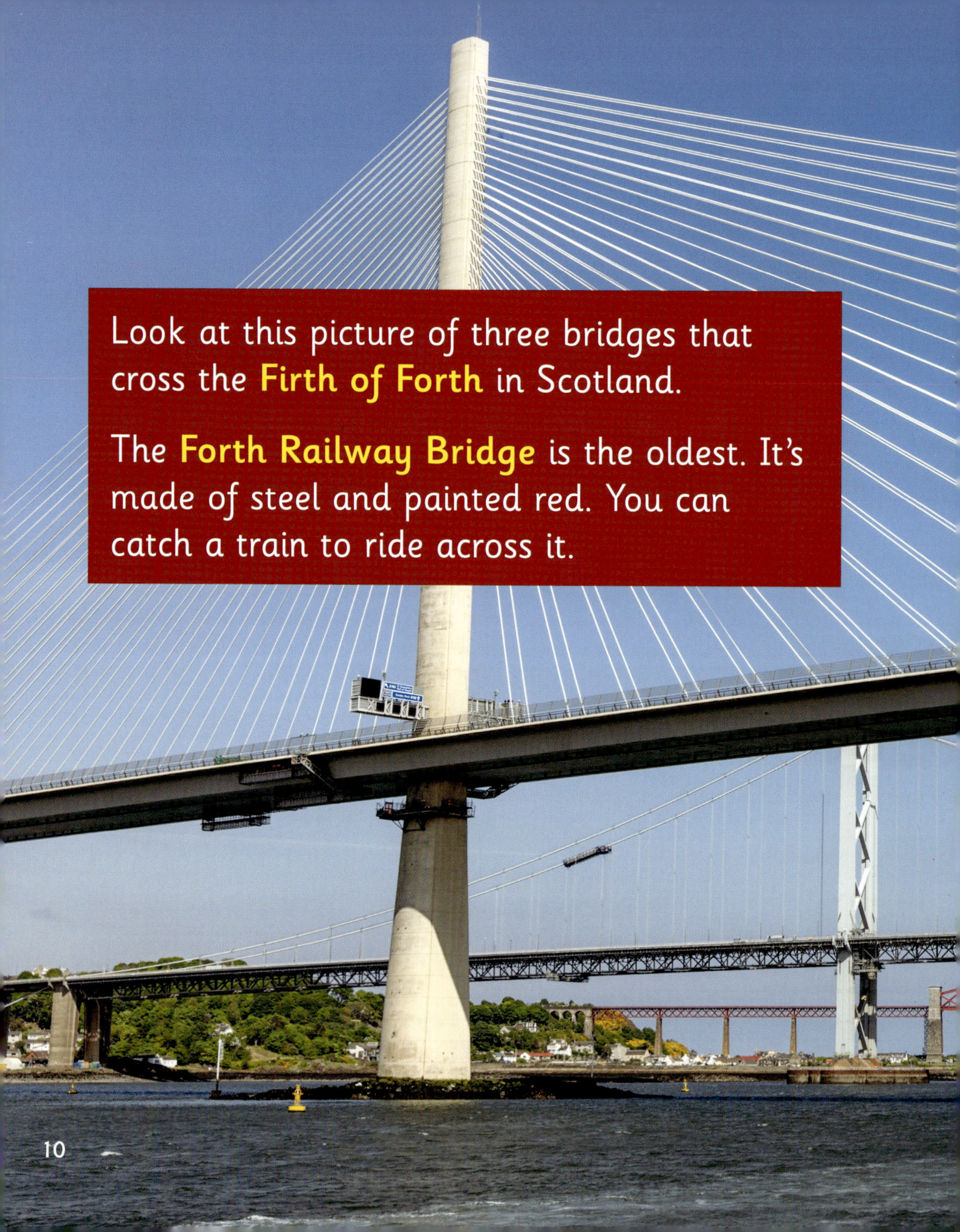

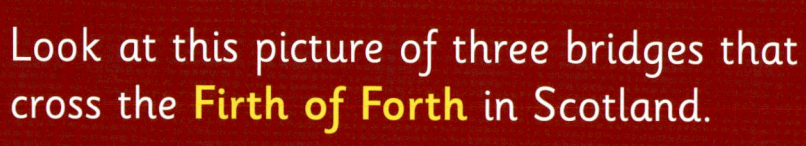

Look at this picture of three bridges that cross the **Firth of Forth** in Scotland.

The **Forth Railway Bridge** is the oldest. It's made of steel and painted red. You can catch a train to ride across it.

The **Forth Road Bridge** was completed about fifty years ago. Cars, trucks and buses cross the bridge, but there is too much traffic for one bridge.

So a third bridge, the **Queensferry Crossing**, was completed a few years ago.

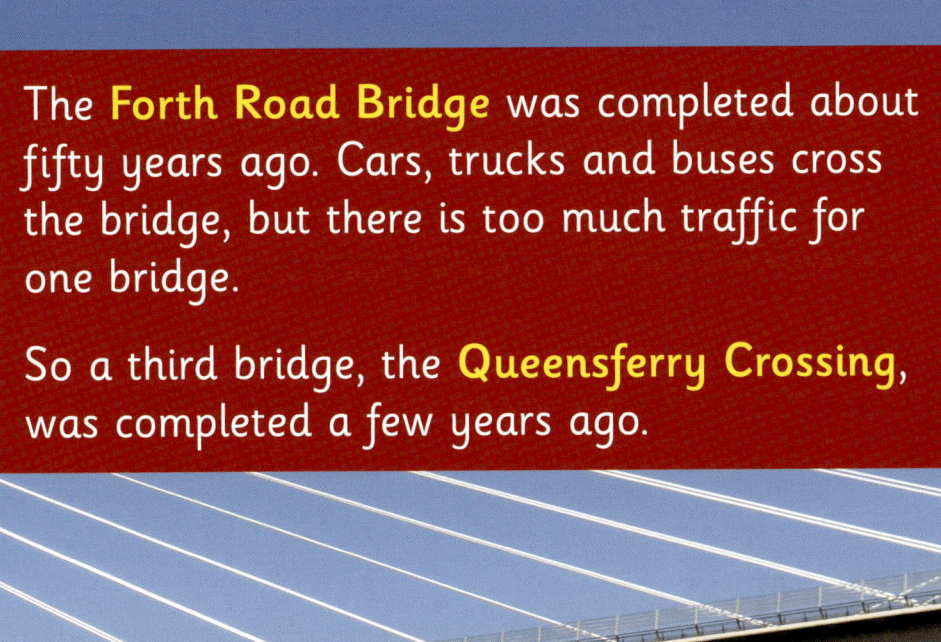

This bridge has a nickname. It's **The Coat Hanger**. Do you think it looks like one?

It would be quite an adventure to climb to the very top of the bridge. You would see a long way from there!

This is one of the longest bridges on the planet. It is over thirty miles long!

Where is it? It is in **China**.

Some bridges are big and grand, but some are small.

This bridge is across a ditch. Mind you don't slip over the edge!

This bridge is over a maze made of hedges.

Is this lamb going to cross this bridge?

These bridges are fantastic too! They are all quite dramatic.

What are they made of? Which one do you like best?